Bucket and Spade

Cockleshell Bay is a town near the sea,
With seagulls and sunshine and sand.
There are shops that sell ices and bright-coloured kites
That fly from a string in your hand.
There are white-painted houses along the sea front,
Where folk come for a quiet holiday,
And the sky is bright, the winds are light,
and two children stay.
So meet – Robin and Rosie of Cockleshell Bay.

Story by Brian Trueman
from the Cosgrove Hall series

Characters designed by Bridget Appleby
Backgrounds drawn by Avril Turner

The Cockle family was moving into their new house by the sea.
"Why did we have to move?" asked Rosie. "I liked our old house."
"Because Dad didn't want to work in a factory any longer," said Robin, "and Mummy doesn't want to live in a town."

Their Dad came out of the house with a pile of rubbish.
"Can you lift the lid off the dustbin for me?"
Robin and Rosie both shouted, "Yes, let *me* do it,"
and pulled at the lid.
"Stop that fighting!" said Mr Cockle, crossly. "Do it *together!*"
And they did. Then Robin asked: "Can we go to the beach?"
"Not today. You don't know the way." Mr Cockle went inside.

Then Mrs Cockle came out – and *she* was carrying rubbish too.
"Can we go to the harbour?" asked Robin,
as he and Rosie lifted the dustbin lid together.
"Not today. You don't know the way, and I'm too busy to take you. Why not play in the garden?"
And *she* went inside.

"Grown ups are always too busy," said Rosie, crossly.
"What shall we do?" said Robin.
"I don't know," said Rosie.
He sat on a crate feeling fed-up. But then Rosie had an idea. "Let's be removal men!"

They found a big cardboard box, and looked
for things to put in it. They found some plates, and their
wellington boots, and there was still room for a nice
shiny kettle, a tea towel, a packet of biscuits, and half
a brick they found in the garden.
The box was very heavy. Rosie couldn't lift it.
Robin tried, and he couldn't either. They tried to
slide it along. Rosie pulled and Robin pushed
but it kept getting stuck on the rough bits in the path.

Suddenly the cardboard tore. Rosie fell over and Robin tripped.
As they lay there, panting a bit, they heard a strange voice.
"Whatever are you doing?" It was a lady they didn't know.
"We're removing," said Rosie.
"Dear me! You've only just arrived!"
"Who are you?" said Robin.
"I'm Mrs Routy, but everyone calls me 'Gran Routy' because I've got eleven grandchildren."

"I've come to help your mother with the guest house," she continued.
"What's a guest house?" asked Rosie.
"It's like a small hotel, where people come for a holiday. It's where you live too. This is going to be a guest house."
"Oh!" said Robin and Rosie together.
"Now, no more questions," said Mrs Routy, knocking on the door.

Mrs Cockle came to the door. "Hello, Mrs Routy.
I'm so glad you're here. Come inside and have a cup of tea."
They both went in, and Robin and Rosie were alone again.
Then Rosie said, "Look. It's not another garden next door.
It's a funny place."

It *was* a funny place, too, if you're used to gardens all in a row.
It was a yard, with a funny old wooden shed that had planks missing.
Inside, they could see coils of rope, and step ladders, and
tins of paint.

"Look," said Rosie. "There's a boat, too."
It was a big one. Because it wasn't in the sea, they could see all the parts of the boat that are usually under water. But, like the shed, some of its planks were missing. There was a ladder leaning against it.

"Look," said Robin. "There's a pair of boots sticking out from under the boat."
"And there's feet in those boots, and legs on the feet, and me on the legs," said another voice they didn't know.
And the boots and legs, and Mr Ship came out from underneath the boat.

"Mr Ship – that's my name," he said.
"Well . . . Mr Shipham really,
but everyone calls me Mr Ship."
"Like they call Mrs Routy 'Gran'," said Robin.
"Ah! So you've met her," said Mr Ship. "What are
your names?" Robin and Rosie told him.
"Robin and Rosie Cockle, eh?
That's a good name for Cockleshell Bay folk."

"When did you arrive?" he asked.
"Today," said Robin and Rosie together.
"As long ago as that!" said Mr Ship. "Well, you'll be wanting to meet *everyone* here, then. Come and meet Fury."
And Mr Ship led them to a little shed on its own in a corner of the yard.

He pulled out a lump of sugar from his pocket
and held it in the palm of his hand.
A furry face came to the door of the shed. It was a donkey.
But just then they heard a shout:
"Robin! Rosie! Time for lunch!"

"Hang on," said Mr Ship. "Before you go...",
and he went to the shed.
He came back with two buckets and spades.
"You can't live at the seaside
without a bucket and spade. They go together."
"Ooh! Thank you!"

Back at home, Mr and Mrs Cockle and Gran Routy were in the sitting-room.
"Phew!" said Mr Cockle. "That's everything away."
"Is this a guest house, now we've moved in?" asked Rosie.
"Well . . . yes," said Mrs Cockle, "and there will be people staying."
"And you'll need a *name* for it," said Gran Routy.

"I'd forgotten that," said Mr Cockle. "How about 'High Tide'?"
"But people might think the tide came into the house," said Mrs Cockle. "How about 'The Anchor'?"
"There's a hotel called that on the other side of town," said Gran Routy. "People might go there instead. That won't do."

Rosie looked at Robin.
"Do you remember what Mr Ship said? About the seaside and buckets and spades always going together. Well, that's what we could call the guest house!"

They held up their buckets and spades. "Look what Mr Ship gave us!"
"We could call our guest house 'The Bucket and Spade'!"
Mr and Mrs Cockle looked at each other.
"What a nice idea! Let's!"

And they all sat down to lunch – in 'The Bucket and Spade' Guest House.

Rosie has hidden the two buckets and spades.
Robin is trying to find them.
Can you help him?

This Thames Magnet edition first published in Great Britain 1985
by Methuen Children's Books Ltd
11 New Fetter Lane, London EC4P 4EE
in association with Thames Television International Ltd
149 Tottenham Court Road, London W1P 9LL
Copyright © 1982 Cosgrove Hall Productions Ltd
Printed in Great Britain
ISBN 0 423 015605
Cockleshell Bay is a Cosgrove Hall Productions film series
The Cockleshell Bay stories were first produced
as single short stories by Marks and Spencer p.l.c.